[signature: Chris Slack]

WHY I'M WINNING

Start Winning Today!

by CHRIS SLACK

Award Winning Sales & Marketing Rep.

xulon
PRESS

Why I'm Winning
Start Winning Today!
by Chris Slack Award Winning Sales & Marketing Rep.

Photo credit: Leinea Nabayan www.leinea.com

Printed in the United States of America.

ISBN 9781545601501

www.xulonpress.com

Dedications

To Lisa, the love of my life: Thanks for believing in me and helping me to finish this book. You have been there through the good times and the bad times. I thank God for creating you just for me. I am truly loved by God and grateful for this incredible life I am living. I look forward to us continuing this extraordinary life together in Christ.

To my son, Chris Jr.: I am very proud of the person you are becoming and the things you have accomplished already as a young man. Your future is bright, and I am thankful for the privilege of watching you continue to win in life.

To my parents Harry Williams Jr. and my mother Orietta Williams: I am so grateful to you, Mom, for always praying for me and always supporting me, correcting me as needed, and never giving up on me when I was on the wrong paths. To Harry Williams Jr., the man who raised me from the age of fifteen to manhood, I can never thank you enough for all the life lessons you not only taught me, but more importantly lived out in front of me. You have shown me how to be a man who takes care of his family just as you did for me, my brother Eddie, and my sister Terrylyn. I thank God to this day for your arrival in our family, and you are the head now who has earned all of our respect and love.

Table of Contents

Forewords

by Kelly Landberg & Janet Louie

"I worked with Chris Slack from 2000 through 2004 at Apria Healthcare, a home medical equipment company. As a Regional Respimed Representative, an inside sales position, Chris sold respiratory medications to our customers. He excelled in this position and was tasked to train others in multiple branches in Southern California. He helped each branch grow their revenue in this product line. An outside Sales Associate position became available, which Chris applied for and was hired.

"Chris did not have any outside sales experience, but was confident that given the opportunity he could succeed. He is very passionate, competitive, and strives to be the best he can be in whatever he does. Chris did not disappoint as he began his outside sales journey. He began in 2002 and the sales numbers did not come in abundance right away, but he had gradual growth. He asked a lot of questions and was always eager to learn new sales techniques. He began to read books on sales and leadership to improve himself. His sales numbers continued to climb. Chris was recruited by LifeCare Solutions in 2004, with an offer he could not turn down. He thanked me for the opportunities that Apria Healthcare provided him, as he resigned in my office in 2004. I understood his position and wished him well and let him know if things changed he would always be welcomed back.

"As chance would have it, I was also recruited by LifeCare Solutions a year later, and I also accepted the job and became the new Vice President of Sales. Chris and I began to work together once again. I saw Chris continue to grow and win in his sales role. After only two years, Chris won Account Manager of the Year in 2006 and again in 2010. Chris was promoted to Sr. Account Manager in 2010. I was there to witness Chris win back to back to back, 2012, 2013, 2014 Account Manager of the Year and present him with those well-deserved awards. He loves to inspire and motivate others to win. He continues to be a tremendous asset to our sales team and is always on the top of our sales leader board.

"If you are looking for positive energy to inspire others, he has enough to go around.

Congratulations Chris on your new book; I wish you much success in all that you do in life!"

-Kelly Landberg
Vice President of Sales
LifeCare Solutions

"I had the opportunity to work with Chris for almost ten years with much of that time spent working closely together to coordinate sales growth and operational management of business in the greater Los Angeles market. Chris came into a company that had recently emerged from bankruptcy with a very narrow business base. He worked diligently to expand the breadth and depth of the products and services we provided to our growing customer base. He managed contractual relationships and was very successful in expanding the scope of business generated from these agreements while also identifying new avenues for generating business and cultivating new affiliations in the market. He has always maintained a solid position among the sales leaders in the company, was often recognized at our annual awards banquet, and was named Salesperson of the Year for three consecutive years.

"Chris is an enthusiastic 'people person' who understands the importance of relationships in both internal and external interactions. He is very perceptive and is able to connect with people and tap into the right motivation to bring out the best in those around him whether it is a member of the operational staff needed to support his customers, a sales associate on his team, or an external customer who has business needs he is looking to fulfill. He has been able to maintain solid working relationships even as business grew and changed, the customer base multiplied, and the external regulatory and compliance environment transformed.

"Chris seems to find joy in learning and sharing his knowledge with others. He works hard to understand the business environment, develop a strategy, and then determine the best way to get those around him excited about the endeavor and willing to work hard to achieve the goals. I am excited to see that he is sharing his expertise with a broader base."

-Janet Louie
Former Chief Operating Officer
LifeCare Solutions

Prologue

I am having so much fun winning at sales and marketing in the healthcare industry, I thought it was time to write and share what I have learned. I believe the principles I have presented in this book will work no matter what you feel gifted or called to do in life. You can be a winner! I hope to inspire everyone who reads this book to know you can accomplish anything you diligently strive after if you develop a never quit attitude and have faith in God our Creator.

If you do not believe in God as the Creator as I do, His laws still work if you apply them. If you work smart and hard, you will be rewarded at some point. It is what I call the spiritual law of sowing and reaping. If you go to work out in the gym to become fit and put in the time, you will get fit. You will reap the benefits of working out from sowing or spending time in the gym. So the story of my career in sales and marketing in the medical equipment field and my successes prove this law of sowing and reaping really works!

One thing I know for sure,
God is 100 percent for your success.

Chapter 1

The Winning Foundation

Train up a child in the way he should go,
And when he is old he will not depart from it.
(Proverbs 22:6)

My life started in New Orleans, Louisiana, where I grew up with my brother Eddie and my sister Terrylyn. My mother, Orietta was eighteen and my father, Robert Reimonenq, was only sixteen when I was born. After my mom and dad split up, my mother married Eddie Slack Sr. He adopted me when I was just a young child and was a good father to us for many years. Though he and my mom divorced when I was twelve years old, I do remember that he loved me and instilled in me the desire to win in life.

> **Eddie Slack Sr. told me, "Son, you can be anything you want to be in this world, even the President of the United States of America."**

However, life became very hard for my family after the divorce. We lived in a very tough, mostly black neighborhood. Since I am a very light skinned mixture of African-American, Cuban, French, and Italian descent, I was bullied because I looked "different." In New Orleans we are called Creole. Those were very hard times for me, but it made me tough. Though I am generally an easy going person who never liked violence, I learned the hard way I had to fight the bully or never get any respect. My childhood friend Marlene said, "Chris, you must fight back." A few fights later in my youth, I earned my respect and the bullying stopped.

> **Those experiences in that tough environment growing up helped me to develop a never quit attitude in all areas of my life.**

Now my mother was a tough lady who ruled her home with an iron fist. She worked two and sometimes three jobs at a time to make the rent and put food on the table. I am grateful to my mother who taught me it takes hard work, discipline, and focus to get what you need and want out of life.

> *She is clothed with strength and dignity,*
> *and she laughs without fear of the future.*
> *When she speaks, her words are wise,*
> *and she gives instructions with kindness.*
> *She carefully watches everything in her household*
> *and suffers nothing from laziness.*
> *Her children stand and bless her....*
> (Proverbs 31:25-28 NLT)

Times were hard until my mother married Harry Williams. He was a godsend who took on her three kids and loved us as his own. However, I was sixteen at the time and full of anger and rebellion for many reasons. Harry talked to me about life many times, but how he lived his life and loved and treated my mother set an example that slowly impacted my life for the better.

Harry worked in the shipping industry and often held down two jobs to provide for his ready-made family. Though he was my stepfather by legal title, I am grateful for the example he gave me as a "father" and for showing me that winning takes hard work, determination, discipline, and focus. I tell everyone that I have a mother and "father" who are the best parents in the world. I also now have a great relationship with Robert, my birth father. I thank the Lord that all old past pains have been healed by His love.

Harry Williams Jr. showed me that hard work, determination, discipline, and focus are necessary to win in life.

---

*Don't you realize that in a race everyone runs, but only one person gets the prize? **So run to win!** All athletes are disciplined in their training. They do it to win a prize that will fade away, but we do it for an eternal prize.* (1 Corinthians 9:24-25 NLT emphasis added)

Developing My Winning Work Ethic

My work history started at a very young age. My first job was delivering newspapers at the age of twelve. My next job was stocking groceries at a local market. At the age of eighteen, I graduated from high school. Though I did give college a try, I regret I allowed the nonstop party atmosphere of New Orleans to keep me from finishing what I started. If I could go back in time, I would make a college degree a priority. Nonetheless, I was determined to make something of myself.

I did some house painting for a while after high school. However, that work was not always steady, so I started looking for more permanent employment. A friend I grew up with said, "Try this restaurant," where he worked. I got hired at a famous restaurant called Pascal's Manale in New Orleans. I was nineteen at that time and really enjoyed working there. The money was not the main reason I liked working there. It was the people that I worked with and the customers who made it a great place to work. This was the beginning of me developing my work ethic.

I started out washing dishes but soon the General Manager promoted me to busman because he saw my strong work ethic and fun outgoing personality. He liked my outgoing fun personality. My duties included bringing them water, cleaning their tables, and doing all that I could to make their customer experience fun and enjoyable. My wage was about $3.50 an hour, and the waitresses would tip me at the end of each shift.

I knew if I took great care of my customers the tips would grow.

I made decent tips at times especially during the Sugar Bowl which was held in New Orleans every year. Thousands of people would come to New Orleans for this event. Our restaurant was Italian cuisine, and we were known for our great barbecued shrimp. The customers had to wear a bib and use hot towels after eating this dish. You had to peel the shrimp and dip them in the sauce that had a fabulous taste, then you would dip the great New Orleans French bread in the same sauce.

One of my favorite perks working there was meeting so many famous people. I met George Burns, Patti La Belle, Joe Montana, Walter Payton, Stephanie Mills, Marla Gibbs, and many others. I developed great people skills serving such a variety of customers. Talking to them about what they were doing made me begin to dream about what I was meant to do with my life. I was not born rich or famous, but I already knew working hard would pay off later in life.

The people I worked with were very cool. There was this guy, called big Chris, who became my best friend. We began hanging out at night; partying, dancing and having lots of fun with girls. Then in 1983, I met and fell in love with a very classy young lady who was raised in a great home. After a few years of dating, I proposed to Lisa and we married in June of 1986. I joined the US Army after

Lisa became pregnant. I wanted to have a secure job to provide for my growing family. We packed up and moved to Fort Hood, Texas.

Military Training

The military was a great place for me to learn teamwork, how to overcome adversity, and win at all cost. Receiving that direct deposit check twice a month from the military gave me a sense of financial security. The military taught me how to handle stress at its highest level. I am a Gulf War Veteran from the 1st Cavalry Division in Fort Hood, Texas; and that experience changed me in ways only a person who has served in a war would truly understand. It gave me a passionate love for God, family, and country.

> **I salute all the service members for what they do to keep us safe. I love my country and am thankful I was able to serve for eleven years.**

Prior to my deployment to Desert Storm, my marriage was not doing well. Lisa decided to take our son and relocate to Buena Park, California. We were separated for a while and divorce was even discussed. Serving in a war affects more than the soldiers. After serving six months in the Gulf War, I was sent back to my base in Fort Hood, Texas.

As Lisa and I are both Christians, a lot of prayer went into the decision for us to reunite. We decided to try and make our marriage work again. In August 1991, I requested a transfer to Fort Ord, California. Thereafter, I made several weekend trips to be with my family. Lisa, our son, and I moved into a small two-bedroom apartment as we worked on rebuilding our marriage and family.

In September of 1992, my Commander explained that the Fort Ord base was scheduled to be closed by the Department of Defense as a military downsizing was ordered by President Bill Clinton. I was offered an early out or I could choose to go to Seoul, Korea, for a twelve-month tour without my family.

With our family just getting back on track, Lisa and I decided to take the early out program. I was given $8,000 and an honorable discharge. Lisa had a job as a Human Resource Secretary at a company called FHP Healthcare. On November 5, 1992, I left the military to start life without the Army and no job.

I was concerned about taking care of my family, but I had enough faith in God to make this bold move.

Winning Key Points

➢ Eddie Slack Sr. told me, "Son, you can be anything you want to be in this world, even the President of the United States of America."

➢ Those experiences in that tough environment growing up helped me to develop a never quit attitude in all areas of my life.

➢ Harry Williams Jr. showed me that hard work, determination, discipline, and focus are necessary to win in life.

➢ Working at the restaurant taught me if I took great care of my customers the tips would grow.

➢ The military was a great place for me to learn teamwork, how to overcome adversity, and win at all cost.

➢ I was concerned about providing for my family, but I had enough faith in God to make this bold move.

➢ One thing I know for sure, God is 100 percent for your success.

Chapter 2

The Winning Beginning

Wayne Gretzky says, "You miss 100 percent of the shots you don't take."

I spent several months on unemployment before finding a job. The first job I was offered was a Security Guard job. I was all ready to take the job offer, but Lisa said, "Don't take that job, God has something better." I was like, "Woman, I need a job, money is running low." Then I got into prayer, agreed with Lisa, and turned the job down. I trusted that the Lord would open a different door as I had several résumés out there. I would be a liar if I said I was at total peace with that decision.

I had sent one of my résumés to FHP Healthcare. The day after I prayed and agreed with Lisa to turn down the Security Guard job offer, I was making dinner, praying, and just waiting for a phone call from someone for an interview or job offer. It was Friday evening at about 5:15 p.m. when the phone rang and the HR Rep for FHP Healthcare offered me a job to be a mail clerk for the company.

I delivered interoffice mail for corporate executives and staff. I have always had a fun personality and was not afraid to talk to anyone. I am blessed from God to be a genuine and sincere person and many people I encounter detect it. I took a part-time second job also selling ladies shows for Robertsons-May, now Macy's. I remembered that my mom and dad both worked two jobs.

Proverbs 10:4 says, "He who has a slack hand becomes poor, but the hand of the diligent makes rich."

We all need to find out what our gift is from God and make the best of it. It's kind of funny that my last name is Slack, but when it came to work, I never believed in slacking off no matter what job I was doing. No pun intended. The examples of hard work from my mom and dad really stuck with me in adulthood. My mother planted a seed in me as a young boy when she told me, "Son, whatever you do for a living be the very best at it, and it will pay off and take you places." I also remember my mom saying, "Son, whatever you put your mind to you can do it, and never let anyone tell you that you can't." I took all those teachings and my early work experiences along with my military training, and applied them to my jobs. I maximized what was deposited in me, knowing that God was going to help me to develop the gifts He had placed within me.

I really enjoyed that job because of all the great and interesting people I got to meet. I was making $8.28 an hour and happy to have found a job. I made up my mind to be the best mail clerk in the company. I became very efficient and was liked by everyone. I was promoted to a different job as a customer service representative in six months. The company was full of great opportunities for people with or without college degrees.

My new job at FHP Healthcare was to admit and discharge patients from Fountain Valley Hospital in Orange County, California. I was not very good at using computers, but I was ready to make more money and learn new things about corporate America. Who you know does make a difference. I have heard it said that one day of favor from the Lord is worth a thousand days of labor. A very nice lady named Marsala Gibson who I went to church with, gave me this new job opportunity. I am forever grateful to her. I started the job and struggled for a while. My sweet wife would go to work with me on Saturdays and Sundays to help me finish reports and show me how to use the computer systems. I taught myself how to type which helped a lot. I liked the challenge, but in the long run the job did not fit me. Sometimes we have to work at one job until the right one becomes available.

The lesson I learned here was to never take a job just for the money unless it is something you need to do until what you want to do shows up.

Since Lisa worked for the company also, she would let me know about other jobs as they became available. Lisa informed me of a job as a Medical Equipment Technician. This job required medical equipment training and experience in working with various pieces of medical equipment. I had some experience from the military in working with heavy equipment and driving heavy vehicles. I applied for the job and presented myself well during the interview. I got the job and my pay went up to $11.21/hr in October, 1994.

Napoleon Hill said, "Whatever the mind of a man can conceive and believe, it can achieve."

I put it in my mind that I could do the job, convinced the interviewer that I could do it, and I got the job. I was very happy with the pay, the job, and the new challenge. I started at the bottom on that team cleaning the equipment with a heavy duty water sprayer and various solvents. After a few weeks, I started some great additional training. Having inside connections can get you in the door, but once in the door it's up to you to become a winner and make yourself valuable to the company. One of the ways to do that is to take advantage of any training offered to increase your knowledge of the company and products you are working with.

Employers look for employees who are willing to better themselves. I learned all types of new things about medical equipment. I received training on oxygen machines, nebulizers for asthma patients, hospital beds, and special mattresses to help heal patients with bed sores, walkers, bedside commodes, and so on. I was like a kid in a candy store and life was good.

We moved our family into a bigger and better apartment as money was much better. I became one of the top drivers in that department within the first year on that job. I had worked hard and was passionate about doing my job well and giving my customers excellent service. I felt good about setting up patients with the medical equipment knowing my work was helping them recover from all types of illnesses in the home setting. I worked a lot of overtime and earned even more money.

Things were going so well financially that Lisa and I decided it was time to buy a house. We began to look around and found a nice townhouse for a good price. I did that job for several years and then a layoff came up because our company was bought out by a competitor in December, 1996. The timing could not have been worse after buying a house. I went on unemployment and started the job search once again.

A friend of mine at the church I was attending had a window cleaning service company. He washed windows for local businesses in nearby cities. His truck was not working, so he offered me a job helping him out until his truck was repaired. I provided him with transportation and also helped out by washing windows. He paid me $25/day. I had fun doing it. I knew I needed to work, and I did whatever it took to make money to help our situation.

Then I applied for a job at Apria Healthcare and was hired as a customer service representative. My job was to take orders for medical equipment over the phone and to set up home and hospital deliveries for patients. I was now on the other side of the business. I had all the hands-on knowledge of the medical equipment, so this job was a good fit for me. I also received more pay than the last job.

My new wage was $13.50/hr. My supervisor Taffy and lead Angela taught me how to use the computers for this job. It was challenging once again, but I caught on. I appreciate them both to this day.

I worked to be the best I could be and a year and half later I was promoted to Regional Respiratory Representative, an inside sales job. I was given a phone script and a week of training on the sales pitch. I learned to call total strangers and was able to offer them a service in a way that just made perfect sense to them. Now, I did not get every customer, but I did do very well. The job came with a nice $2.00 pay raise, too. My previous work experiences were paying off from working in New Orleans restaurants, selling ladies' shoes, delivering groceries for Albertsons part time, and being a driver with hands-on experience with the medical equipment. God was putting it all together!

My wife was laid off a few times during those years. So I stepped up and worked two jobs for a while until she found something. While working for FHP as a driver and then working for Apria Healthcare, I delivered groceries for Albertsons part time in the evenings. Those were long days with little sleep, but my family needed me to provide. My parents and the military taught me that with discipline, hard work, and a can-do winning attitude, I could make it no matter what I was doing. These were the foundations that kept pushing me to win and be the best I could be. I would often call my mom and dad and tell them how the things they taught me were paying off. They were very proud of my accomplishments.

One of the main reasons why I was winning was because my day started off with an attitude of gratitude and thankfulness to the Lord for all I currently have.

As far as the job goes, I put the customer first and always did my very best to give 100 percent all the time. My sales numbers grew month to month, and my boss was very pleased with my results. Soon I was charged with training customer service teams in eleven other branches on how to sell respiratory medications to customers who had our nebulizer machines, but received their medications from other pharmacies. The staff members in these other branches began to capture more of the market share of the respiratory medications as well. I would go to each location monthly to reinforce the training and help the growth of this product line.

I did that job for about eighteen months. Then I heard that an outside sales position had opened up in July of 2002. I went to my boss Gary and inquired about the position, and his first reply to me was I did not have any outside sales experience. He was correct as far as the Healthcare Industry was concerned, but I felt very confident I could do the job because I had sold ladies' shoes face to face and did very well at that sales job. I felt ready to go out in the field to sell all the medical equipment and products I had previously sold over the phone.

After bugging the Area Sales Manager to give me a chance, Gary finally gave me the opportunity. I went for it with 100 percent effort, enthusiasm, and focus. I would tell myself, "I am going to make this happen and be good at it."

The mind is a powerful tool when aligned with focus, passion, and determination.

I am forever grateful to Gary for giving me that opportunity. I knew I could do sales and marketing because of my ability to connect with people. I learned that I had this gift based on my prior jobs and successes.

Babe Ruth said, "Every strike brings me closer to my next home run."

The Power of a Winning Mind-set

Though I have had many customers say, "I'm not inter-ested," my **winning mind-set** continued to move me ahead. In sales you only have a small window to start generating referrals and revenue. Most companies give you three to six months to start seeing positive results; otherwise you will probably be let go. Sales people either bring in the business or at some point it's over. That being said, you can learn to sell if you really apply yourself and don't quit.

When I began this outside sales job, I was given two weeks of training and off I went. I had to learn how to open up and develop a new sales territory. I can tell you that it is not an easy task. I started to read sales books on how to do it. Those self-help books really paid off. In fact, I still read two or three books a year to stay sharp. My mind needed to be filled with sales techniques; therefore, I put in the time and effort to get the knowledge I needed.

When you want something to happen, you need to take the appropriate actions to reach your goals. To be a winner, it will cost you something, but it will pay off in the long run and set you apart. Selling is a skillset that you can acquire over time. For me, talking to people comes easy. However, I also know when trying to sell something you only have a few seconds to get and keep the customer's attention. To do that takes fine tuning, persistence, and the right mind-set.

Proverbs 23:7 says, "For as he thinks in his heart, so is he."

The Greek word for "heart" in this verse actually means the mind, not your beating heart. You need to see yourself being successful before it comes; then let your actions back up what you see in your mind. Your hard work and gifts will make doors open for you.

I know it works because that is what happened to me. My name was getting out there in the sales world, and a few years later I was recruited by Lifecare Solutions. Unbeknownst to me, my co-worker Harry was recruited as well. This was in April of 2004. We both met with Tom, the CEO, and interviewed on the same day in San Diego, California. I took the great offer Lifecare Solutions made.

I gave my letter of resignation to my VP of Sales, Kelly Landberg. It was a sad but happy day; I made the move I thought was best for me and my family. Kelly was gracious and understanding and wished me well. She was a class act then and still is to this day.

I showed up for work at my new job on April 19, 2004, and ran into Harry. I was shocked and happy at the same time. We both got hired, but did not know it. We were going from Apria Healthcare, a huge national company, to Lifecare Solutions which was a small company that had just come out of bankruptcy in 2003. Tom had been hired as CEO to turn the company around. Janet Louie was the GM at the Pasadena branch at that time where both Harry and I were assigned. The branch was not dead, but definitely needed some new blood. It had no sales reps as they had both quit shortly before Harry and I were hired. The branch had two customer service reps and two drivers.

At first, Harry and I wondered what we had gotten ourselves into, but that lasted for just a few moments. We knew we were about to embark on a new sales journey and help the Pasadena branch and Lifecare Solutions turn around and grow its revenues. I prayed a lot and also knew that I needed the favor of God to grow that sales area and convince large medical groups to follow me to this company. The good news was, Lifecare Solutions had some nice contracts on the books that I already had relationships with. The bad news was the contracts were not generating much revenue. Harry and I said it was time to make things happen in our respective sales areas, and we set out to do just that!

Winning Key Points

➢ Wayne Gretzky says, "You miss 100 percent of the shots you don't take."

➢ Proverbs 10:4 says, "He who has a slack hand becomes poor, but the hand of the diligent makes rich."

➢ We all need to find out our gift from God and then make the best of it.

➢ My mother planted a seed in me as a young boy, "Son, whatever you do for a living be the very best at it, and it will pay off and take you places."

➢ I also remember my mom saying, "Son, whatever you put your mind to you can do it, and never let anyone tell you that you can't."

➢ I learned to never take a job just for the money unless it is something you need to do until what you want to do shows up.

➢ Napoleon Hill said, "Whatever the mind of a man can conceive and believe, it can achieve."

➢ I can tell you one of the main reasons I was winning was because I started my day with an attitude of gratitude and thankfulness to the Lord.

➢ As far as the job goes, I put the customer first and always did my very best to give one hundred percent all the time.

- ➤ The mind is a powerful tool when aligned with focus, passion, and determination.
- ➤ Babe Ruth said, "Every strike brings me closer to my next home run."
- ➤ Proverbs 23:7 says, "For as he thinks in his heart, so is he".
- ➤ You need to see yourself being successful before it comes; then let your actions back up what you see in your mind.

Chapter 3

The Winning Challenge

**Quote from Proverbs 18:15, "Intelligent people
are always ready to learn. Their ears are
open for knowledge" (NLT).**

M y new journey with Lifecare Solutions medical
equipment began in Los Angeles and Pasadena,
California, where my branch was located. I had a large
sales area with a lot of potential, but also a lot of challenges
and competitors to go with it. At this time in my life, I was
still learning how to develop a sales territory.

I can tell you that opening up a new sales area can be
very intimidating for a fairly new sales rep like I was. Since
I was still a rookie, I said to myself, "It's time to read and
get more knowledge on how to develop a new sales area." I
learned this process can take up to six months or even more

to really cultivate and make the right connections with all the major potential referral sources.

I had to develop a system to make the call cycles make sense for my customers and my company.

So I worked it out where each day I called on customers in certain areas. This allowed me to maximize my time and efforts. However, I found that some customers only allow sales calls on certain days and times. As I began to understand this, I had to make some adjustments so I could make sales calls to certain customers on certain days a few times per month.

I knew after six months how to focus more on my 20 percent who gave me 80 percent of my business. As I continued to hone in on my sales skills, a wise Account Manager I know gave me a test that his old boss had given him. He said, "Chris, sell me this cell phone." I began to tell him all the great features and benefits about the cell phone and he stopped me cold. He said, "Chris, you failed the test. You jumped right in and tried to sell me something without first asking me what I was looking for." A light bulb went off in my head and I said, "I blew this one."

> **Then the Account Manager said something that has stayed with me ever since, "Chris, telling is not selling."**

It was a valuable lesson I will never forget. Another important lesson I learned in those first few months was preparation is essential to success. Obviously, you cannot anticipate every possible scenario, but the more you study and put into practice the knowledge you gain, the better prepared you can be when facing your existing and potential customers.

> **Michael Jordan once said, "Preparation eliminates fear."**

I am a huge Michael Jordan fan and have gleaned many words of wisdom from this great athlete. He said in an interview with Ahmad Rashad that he is ready to make the big shots because in practice he does them over and over until he feels confident he can make them. Then, when that winning moment comes in a real live game, he is not afraid or nervous because of the many hours of preparation (during practice) that he already did before ever standing in front of the opposing teams. He has made and missed many, but it only drives a champion like him to continue to prepare for the next big moment. Sales is no different. In fact, any goal you want to reach requires the same level of commitment and preparation to achieve the victory.

John C. Maxwell says it best in his books that "Talent is never enough."

He explains that gifted people who think their gifts and talents are enough without continuing to improve themselves will get passed up by people with less talent who out-work them. Sales people, athletes, and many other careers would fall under this quote. When I started with Lifecare Solutions, I was at the very bottom of the rankings for a while. I promised the new CEO that I would bring business with me to Lifecare Solutions. I knew that I needed to develop and improve my gifts and talents of which I had been successful with previously.

Customers are not always willing to change over to other companies even though they like you. I was very blessed to have one major customer give my new company a shot. I moved heaven and earth to make sure every referral they sent received the best customer service possible. I even delivered the products at times to make sure things were done above and beyond what was expected. When you want to win at something bad enough, you will outwork everyone and do jobs that you weren't even hired to do at times. You need to provide a superior level of customer service to keep them coming back.

Sales Strategies for a New Sales Territory

> **John C. Maxwell said, "If we're growing, we're always going to be out of our comfort zone."**

This is how I opened up a new sales territory in the Los Angeles county area which consisted of many potential referral sources in several small cities I had no knowledge of. There are many new innovative ways to apply sales and marketing strategies today. I highly suggest you take my advice and research all the new things that are now available that I did not have or know about when I started in outside sales in 2002. I am always looking for new and better strategies so I can continue to improve and grow.

> **I once heard it said that if you are not growing you are dying. To me, the choice was obvious.**

1. If you have good referral sources from a different sales area you used to work in, see if they know anyone in the sales area you are now trying to break into and ask

for leads and recommendations. Be sure you know what services and products are primary for your company's revenue objectives. This is key in helping you focus on the right types of referral sources.

2. If you are new in sales with no prior referral sources, research the top ten referral sources in the sales areas that do high volume business for the products or services you are selling. Find out what their top three needs are and top three challenges are with companies they currently work with.

3. Find out who are the top three to five competitors in your sales area. Research them to see how they do what they do, how long have they been in the area, their strengths and weaknesses, etc.

4. Use all this information to make your sales and marketing strategies more effective when entering into a new area to grow your business.

5. Study the differences your company has that can better meet the customer's needs. If you find that your company is very similar to the other companies, then get creative and make up something new that will give you a selling edge. Think outside the box as I did when I created my company's first Hospital Liaison position in 2005. Present your ideas to your sales leadership as I did.

Think outside the box.

6. Now you are ready to formulate your sales strategies. Make sales calls by phone, use the search engine technologies to gather names, e-mails, and so on to make your first contact as warm as possible.

7. **Understand the power of face-to-face calls.** Use all the new ways to touch the customers, but I can tell you my face-to-face sales calls are still my number one and most powerful sale's tool. I make a positive connection and build on it weekly in my sales call cycles. You learn the customer's needs and times of availability and build your sales call cycle from that information. **If they have weekly meetings, see if you can attend once a month to see how things are going with the service your company provides.** This will allow you to you become a partner in a manner of speaking, to help resolve any problems that may arise and also get feedback on customer service. The next thing you know, you are invited to their company's Christmas party as a guest. This is exactly what happened to me.

8. You must map out your sales areas daily to see how the traffic flows; this will enable you to make the best plan possible and to maximize your field time

so that your customers are available to meet with you for a few minutes once you arrive. Once you do this, the rest of your day will flow pretty good most of the time. **It is best practice to have a daily plan or you will be unproductive often and see little to no growth.**

The above eight steps were instrumental in me winning my first Account Manager of the Year award for the highest sales score out of about 30 sales representatives. Shortly, thereafter, my co-worker Harry was promoted to Sr. Account Manager and became my boss. He gave me some valuable advice and leadership that propelled my career to a greater level.

Harry once told me that being a great listener was a primary key to selling.

When you listen to the customer talk, you gain valuable information on what they are looking for. I am a natural talker so listening is something I have to continue to remember to do. You may say since you have all this experience and writing a book on sales, shouldn't you have this mastered by now. The answer is yes and no. We all have certain things we master and some things we may master at times. I just want to keep it real and let people know you do not have to be perfect to sell or have every sales technique mastered. Some sales people may rely too much on their talents to carry them and not consider improving themselves and working on their weaknesses.

Know your strengths, continue to improve them, continue to work on your weaknesses and areas that need improvement.

The Winning Speech

Confucius said, "He who says he can and he who says he can't are usually both right."

People who are always complaining or always speaking negative will most likely yield bad or negative results. Our words have power. It's up to us to choose to speak words that build up and create instead of words that will keep us stuck in a rut, broke, sick, and frustrated with our life. To make things even worse, you make people miserable around you, too. People will begin to duck and dodge being around you.

> **Proverbs 18:21 says, "Death and life are in the power of the tongue, and those who love it will eat its fruit."**

This means that what we say has power over our life, so why not speak positive declarations. I have many friends; some study the Bible and some don't. Even the ones who don't, use this principle of positive declarations. Speaking positive and not negative just makes sense to me. For years, I have spoken negative words at times in my life. However, today, 95 percent of my words are positive for my life and others around me.

> **Advice from King David, "This is the day the Lord has made; let us rejoice and be glad in it".**

So the good news is when you begin each day saying, today is a good day and I will make the best of this day, you are on your way to bigger and better things. This will help you to start your day super positive, passion will come out of you, and creativity can now begin to flow. Being a Christian, I give thanks to my heavenly Father and Lord Jesus Christ every morning when I wake up. I start my day being very thankful for everything I already have. It's called the attitude of gratitude.

I am also convinced that the guiding principles for everything we do in life can be found in the Bible, so I spend time daily reading and studying it.

Some people don't even realize they are complaining as much as they do. I have done my share of complaining about things, so I know how bad negative words can add to us continuing to underachieve or just stay stuck where we are in life. You see, our words are super important to becoming a winner. We need to speak positive as often as we can and stay silent until something positive comes to mind. I do my very best to be around positive people. I have the winning mind-set. Speaking positive on a consistent basis is not only healthy for you, but it fuels others around you.

Proverbs 21:23 says, "Whoever guards his mouth and tongue keeps his soul from troubles."

Learn from Defeat

**"I am not one of those who think that
coming in second or third is winning."
– Robert Francis Kennedy**

To win in life we need to use words like:

I can do it, I will make this happen.

I will outwork people who may have more gifts than me.

I will find a way to win.

I will study my craft daily to beat my competitors out.

I am going to be great at whatever I do by hard work,

discipline, focus, and keeping a can-do attitude daily.

I apply these kinds of thoughts and words to my life every day. I have to in order to be the best. I have been in second place in bowling tournaments, sales scores, dominos, cards, darts, billiards, ping pong, you name it. Every time I came in second, I learned something from that experience. Then I knew what to do differently to be number one the next time. In each one of those games or sales competitions that I came in second, I eventually did come in first place.

> **Winning is all about how we prepare, how we think, how we speak, even how we walk, and what type of energy comes off us.**

I radiate high positive energy on a daily basis. We are all human so we will all have moments that life beats us down, but winners always find a way to get back up to fight another day. This is what it takes to win in all areas of our lives.

> **"If you learn from defeat, you haven't really lost."**
> **– Zig Ziglar**

The great basketball hall of famer, Michael Jordan is a great example of a man who had to learn from defeat. He had to fight with the Detroit Pistons for years before he and the Chicago Bulls came out of the Eastern Conference to play for the NBA championship. The Detroit Pistons played a very physical brand of basketball so Jordan said, "I must get stronger to beat these guys." So, in the off season, he hit the gym and got stronger. In 1991, he and the Bulls beat the Detroit Pistons in the Eastern Conference finals and went on to beat Magic Johnson and the Los Angeles Lakers for their first NBA championship. Jordan and the Bulls went on to win three in a row after getting over that wall called the Detroit Pistons. In life we will get knocked down many times, but we should always learn from that setback or defeat.

We are only defeated if we give up.

We should become wiser and ask ourselves what we need to do different to get over this hurdle. Seek advice from a mentor or positive role model. A mentor is someone we trust and look up to. This person will keep it real and tell us the truth even if it does not agree with what we think. Being around people who have learned to work smarter and have reached the goals we are seeking to attain, can be a positive experience. We should consider submitting to others who have strengths in areas we need improvement. I like to be around people who are super positive and have plans to win at whatever they are into.

Winning is all about how you set your mind **to be the best**. I hate second place. There is an old saying that if you are second, then you are the first to lose. I have been there before and reaching first place is what drives me.

"I've learned that something constructive comes from every defeat." – Coach Tom Landry

Winning Key Points

"Any fact facing us is not as important as our attitude toward it, for that determines our success or failure. The way you think about a fact may defeat you before you ever do anything about it. You are overcome by the fact because you think you are." –Norman Vincent Peale

---

➢ Quote from Proverbs 18:15, "Intelligent people are always ready to learn. Their ears are open for knowledge" (NLT).

➢ I had to develop a system to make the call cycles make sense for my customers and my company.

➢ My new boss, Harry said something that has stayed with me ever since, "telling is not selling."

➢ Michael Jordan once said, "Preparation eliminates fear."

➢ John C. Maxwell says it best in one of his *books that "Talent is never enough."*

➢ John C. Maxwell said, "If we're growing, we're always going to be out of our comfort zone."

➢ I once heard it said that if you are not growing you are dying. To me, the choice was obvious.

➢ Think outside the box.

➢ Harry once told me that being a great listener was a primary key to selling.

➢ Know your strengths, continue to improve them, continue to work on your weaknesses and areas that need improvement.

➢ Confucius said, "He who says he can and he who says he can't are usually both right."

➢ Proverbs 18:21 says, "Death and life are in the power of the tongue, and those who love it will eat its fruit."

➢ Advice from King David, "This is the day the Lord has made; let us rejoice and be glad in it."

➢ I am also convinced that the guiding principles for everything we do in life can be found in the Bible, so I spend time daily reading and studying it.

➢ Proverbs 21:23 says, "Whoever guards his mouth and tongue keeps his soul from troubles."

➢ "I am not one of those who think that coming in second or third is winning." – Robert Francis Kennedy

➢ Winning is all about how we prepare, how we think, how we speak, even how we walk, and what type of energy comes off us.

➢ "If you learn from defeat, you haven't really lost." – Zig Ziglar

➢ We are only defeated if we give up.

> ➤ "I've learned that something constructive comes from every defeat." – Coach Tom Landry

Chapter 4

The Winning Drive

> *"Work Hard. Do your best. Keep your word.*
> *Never get too big for your britches.*
> *Trust in God. Have no fear;*
> *and never forget a friend."*
> **–Harry S. Truman**

I want to share my perspective on what I saw and was a part of to help Lifecare Solutions grow from filing for bankruptcy in 2003 to being sold in January of 2011 to Preferred DME for millions. The CEO was Tom, a no-nonsense person. He was known for turning companies around. I met him in April of 2004, in San Diego, California. He interviewed me very extensively and asked me great probing questions. I sold myself and he saw enough potential in me to give me a shot. This company needed revenue growth, new contracts, new sales staff, and so on. Many changes were needed to ensure Lifecare Solutions success for the long-term.

I reached out to my boss from Apria Healthcare, Kelly Landberg, VP of Sales whom I greatly admire to this day. I said, "Hey, Kelly, I would like to work for you again."

She replied, "Are you leaving Lifecare Solutions?"

I said, "No, we have an opening for VP of Sales."

She just starting laughing and so did I. I was recruiting her because our VP of Sales had recently left. I started telling her how it was a place she could help build from the ground up. Then I told her about Tom, our new CEO, who did what made sense and would be open to new ideas if it would help grow our revenue. Kelly was happy for me, but said she was not interested. Well, a month or two later, I received an e-mail that Kelly had been hired as the new VP of Sales and Marketing for Lifecare Solutions. Harry and I both were very pleased to hear this. We knew with Kelly on board the sales team would grow, the revenue would grow, and the company would grow.

The other person Tom put in place was Janet. Janet is as smart as they come. She is a pharmacist by trade and was the GM of the Pasadena branch where Harry and I worked. Tom promoted Janet to VP of Operations in 2006. Tom also interviewed Rene who was the Respiratory Manager at the time for the Pasadena branch. Tom asked Harry and me what we thought about Rene. Our answer was that he was one of the hardest working people we had ever met. Tom hired Rene as the GM to take Janet's place. Other parts of the team were still being built, but the main players were now in place. Tom, Kelly, Janet, Rene, Harry, and myself. The Pasadena branch became one of the company's highest revenue producing branches.

Prayer and a Great Action Plan

Harry and I went to work every day on a mission to secure new contracts and new business. We both focused on several of the accounts we had with the other company. I would pray daily for divine favor, then follow up with a great action plan on how and who to go after for Lifecare Solutions. The winning mind-set was in full focus mode. I said to myself, "I am going to make this happen, I am going to win key accounts and contracts for Lifecare Solutions."

Bit by bit we grew and grew. Harry and I had some very healthy monthly competitions, too. We pushed each other to win, and I made it a point to see what numbers the other Account Managers were doing. The numbers showed that we had some fabulous Account Managers on board. Kelly did her job well by hiring the best of the best:

Laureen, Judy, Marion, Rick, Cheryl, James, Zack, Lance, and many other great sales reps who completed the team. I have learned something from each one of these excellent sales people. Another secret to success is to always maintain a teachable spirit.

> **"Everyone is my teacher. Some I seek.**
> **Some I subconsciously attract.**
> **Often I learn simply by observing others.**
> **Some may be completely unaware that**
> **I'm learning from them, yet I bow**
> **deeply in gratitude." – Eric Allen**

We all worked very hard and we grew. In 2006, we had our first annual Sales Ops leadership meeting in San Diego, California. I won Account Manager of the Year with the highest sales score out of about twenty or so sale reps. I beat out everyone, and it felt great to be number one. I was on cloud nine. The winning mind-set with a game plan and hard work will always pay off. The Bible says you will reap what you sow (2 Corinthians 9:6). I sowed hard work and reaped my reward.

I can tell you it was a close race. Harry won number one for total oxygen starts, and Rick, our San Diego Account Manager, won number one Account Manager of the Year for highest total KFP's (Key Focus Products). My GM Rene was recognized for having the highest percent of revenue growth for the year. It felt even greater knowing my branch had achieved this award. This means as a team, we did our jobs at a very high level for a long period of time, and we grew our revenues at a very rapid pace from 2005 to 2006.

Our great CEO Tom said we were growing at a little over 20 percent a year while the overall industry was growing at about 7 to 8 percent. So what we had accomplished was explosive growth. We had the big momentum working for us now, and it continued to motivate us to even work harder.

So how did we do it? Tom knew how to motivate a sales force. He and Kelly, our VP of Sales, put some great incentives out on the table that would make the sales team some very, very nice commissions. The main incentives were focused on growing our oxygen census. This product line is probably one of our biggest long-term revenue contributors. I can tell you that our oxygen census grew by leaps and bounds in one year. The other companies like ours were growing at 7 to 8 percent a year. This explosive growth went on from 2004 to 2011. Tom, Kelly, and Janet did a great job keeping us motivated and moving forward.

The investment firm who bought Lifecare Solutions out of bankruptcy in July of 2003 for about $4,000,000, sold it eight years later for something like $60 to $70 million. Our great CEO Tom did what he was hired to do and did it very well. Tom is a smart leader. I really learned a lot from him. He had an open door policy, and I was able to speak to him on things as needed. I will always look up to Tom and Janet for giving me the opportunity as an Account Manager with Lifecare Solutions. I continued to learn and grow in my career with the company.

In 2009, I came in second place. My friend and co-worker Cheryl was the number one Account Manager that year. Harry told me I was beat by just a few points. I was in the Philippines on a missionary trip with my church when I found out. I was happy for Cheryl, but I am not one to rejoice in second place.

The winning mind-set will drive me to strive to always be number one.

I love winning at whatever I do. I love to compete and win. Second place is not worth discussing to me. So, when I got back home from that twelve-day mission trip, I told my wife Lisa I was on a new mission. The winning mind-set was in full force with a goal to be number one for 2010.

A famous quote from Buddha says: "The mind is everything. What you think you become."

So with my plan in place and my winning mind-set, I went out and worked hard to bring in new business. My current referral sources grew as well. The KFP's (Key Focus Products) sales grew weekly. We had our 2010 annual sales meeting in San Diego at the corporate office. I tell you, when they called my name it felt really great. I had reached my goal as Account Manager of the Year. This was award number two for me since 2004. My numbers that year were well ahead of everyone. To stay on top takes a lot of personal discipline, mind-set focus, and dedication to your customers. I must say that if sales people don't also show respect for the team of people responsible for delivering the products and services they are selling, they will not enjoy sustained success. Our internal team is just as important as our external customers.

"Do to others as you would have them do to you."
–Jesus Christ[1]

---

[1] Luke 6:31 NIV

I strive to live this way. I make it a point to show respect for all the members on my team. I am part of a team, and we all win together. The Winning Mind-set knows you always have other people to thank for their contribution in your success. Every time I win Account Manager of the Year, I thank the Lord for my blessings, health, and strength. I thank my Pasadena teammates, and I especially thank my wife for her love and support. No one becomes a winner alone. We all need help and can learn from other people. I did not win in 2011, but I came back and won again in 2012, 2013, and 2014.

"The best revenge is massive success."
– Frank Sinatra

Though I grew up poor, living on food stamps at times, and bullied because of the color of my skin, I would not change a thing because it all made me tougher, stronger, and more determined to become a winner. A scene from the movie Rocky where he was discussing boxing and life with his son has always been an inspiration for me. His son had been living in his father's shadow and blamed his father for his lack of success in life. So he did not want Rocky to box again. Rocky said, "Son, you let people stick a finger in your face and tell you that you are a loser or you're not good enough. Then when things got hard, you looked for someone to blame. The world is hard and life will beat you down, but we must take the hits and keep getting back up. Don't sit around and blame others saying you are not where you should be because of him or her or them or your neighborhood. Cowards do that and that's not me. Winners take the hits and keep getting back up and that's how winning is done."

Like Rocky, I live with a "can-do" attitude every day. We will all face adversity in this life, but the secret is to just keep learning, growing, and working hard then our time of winning will come. Focus, discipline, and a winning mind-set will carry us, push us, and drive us to be the best. It all starts in our mind. We must believe in ourselves to become a winner.

The Los Angeles and Pasadena markets are loaded with competition from other medical equipment providers, but my career path has never been better. I know that each one of my referral sources and medical groups get to choose who they give their business to every day. When they choose Lifecare Solutions, it is because of my sales and marketing skills and the team of people at my local branches. The success I am enjoying is because of hard work, a tenacious winning attitude, studying my craft, continuing self-improvement, and lots of prayer for myself and my team.

> **I stay focused, disciplined, set goals, and apply what I have learned. This is my winning formula.**

Nothing was ever just handed to me. I've earned everything I gained in my sales and marketing career. I win because I believe in myself, I work hard, I plan to win, I see myself winning, I seek out advice from other winners, and I read about those who are successful. I trust God for favor as well. I am very grateful to everyone who has poured into my life both professionally and spiritually.

> **I have overcome many challenges in my life to become a winner; you can too.**

Winning Key Points

> ➤ "Work Hard. Do your best. Keep your word. Never get too big for your britches. Trust in God. Have no fear; and never forget a friend." – Harry S. Truman
> ➤ I would pray daily for divine favor, then follow up that prayer with a great action plan.
> ➤ "Everyone is my teacher. Some I seek. Some I subconsciously attract. Often I learn simply by observing others. Some may be completely unaware that I'm learning from them, yet I bow deeply in gratitude." – Eric Allen

➢ The winning mind-set will drive me to strive to always be number one.

➢ A famous quote from Buddha says: "The mind is everything. What you think you become."

➢ "Do to others as you would have them do to you." – Jesus Christ[2]

➢ "The best revenge is massive success." – Frank Sinatra

➢ I stay focused, disciplined, set goals, and apply what I have learned. This is my winning formula.

➢ I have overcome many challenges in my life to become a winner; you can too.

---

[2] Luke 6:31 NIV

Chapter 5

The Winning Process

> "You were born to win, but to be a winner,
> you must plan to win, prepare to win, and
> expect to win."
> – Zig Ziglar

Whenever we embark on a new business, a new job, or a new career, we need to make sure we are matching what we are moving into as closely as possible to our passions and our strongest skill sets. In order to stay on track, we should also have a vision of where we are trying to go. Without a vision, we may find ourselves wandering aimlessly and wasting precious time pursuing things that will not move us toward our success in life. This will cause confusion and frustration in our careers and our lives. In fact, if we do not know where we are going, we won't know when we have arrived. If we don't know what our goal is, how will we know if we have achieved it?

"Failing to plan is planning to fail." –Alan Lakein

A winning vision will help us develop a winning plan. This vision should be the thing that drives our actions and encourages us to press on in spite of what is happening all around us. This vision should line up with our gifts and passions. We need to make sure the vision is written out and clearly defined. We must be intentional in our actions or we will lose the "Big Mo"—momentum. We must be "intentional" about moving steadily toward our winning goals.

To be intentional is to make things happen on purpose through planning, focus, and discipline. According to Webster's Dictionary intentional means a voluntary, deliberate action that is brought about of one's own will. "Voluntary" implies freedom of choice or action without external compulsion. Being intentional shows an awareness of an end to be achieved.

"If you don't design your own life plan, chances are you'll fall into someone else's plan. And guess what they have planned for you? Not much." –Jim Rohn

No matter what we are aiming to do in life, we need to have a focus that pushes us when others may not see what we see. We must not allow others or our circumstances make us give up on pursuing our vision. Sometimes others may be part of working with us toward achieving our goal, but other times we may be alone on our journey to success. When we are alone, it may take us longer to accomplish our vision, but the good news is we have already learned hard work and staying the course will help us get there.

> **"Any idea, plan, or purpose may be placed in the mind through repetition of thought."**
> **–Napoleon Hill**

We will become unstoppable at reaching our goals when we keep our focus on the vision and do only what moves us toward our goal. It takes internal strength and focus to finish the course and achieve success. Some people may start out with us, but only the strong will continue to stand beside us when things are moving slow or things get tough. Still, it is good to have someone we trust to advise us as we explain our plan. They may see something we might not see. Just make sure if others are brought in on this vision and plan that they are high energy, high integrity people.

> **We need the right people in our inner circle to advise and help us complete the goals and attain our vision. "Every man is my superior that I learn from him." – Thomas Carlyle**

Some people seem to just feed on negative thinking or finding a way to think the worst. I prefer to always try and find the positive even when a negative happens to me or to someone around me. We will all face the negative things life throws at us at times, but how we respond to the challenging times will determine how quick we turn that situation around to a positive. I have always tried to learn from negative experiences. They can teach us if we reflect on what happened, how it happened, and what we could have done to avoid the thing from happening in the first place. There will be times when a negative experience will be out of our control, but we can still learn from that as well. If nothing else, it may teach us to be prepared for the unexpected and not let such circumstances keep us from accomplishing our goals.

What we think on is what we will speak about the most, whether it is negative or positive, so voluntarily choose the positive. The Wright brothers thought they could build a vehicle or machine that could fly one day and it became a reality. Thomas Edison thought we could harness electricity one day and it became a reality. A man said, "Let's fly to the moon," and man came up with a way to do it! Nothing is impossible if we can believe it and not doubt. The way to stay focused and continually move forward is to believe, have a strong faith, and a conviction in what we are doing.

By keeping our eyes on the goal and knowing our vision is attainable through hard work and perseverance, we will get there if we do not quit or give up.

Developing a Winning Vision

Winning Point #1: Write Down Your Vision

By writing the vision down, you can see it more clearly.[3] Writing the plan will help you see where you are going and how to get there. As the old saying goes, a picture is worth a thousand words. Once you see it in your heart and mind, it becomes clear as you write it down on paper. Then your faith will cause you to believe that it can be accomplished.

Winning Point #2: Do Your Research

Do lots of research on how to develop a winning plan. This will save you time and money as you move into that plan. Take someone out to lunch who is doing what you desire to do and doing it well. If that's not an option, buy their book and other books to do your research. These days, the internet might be the cheapest and most effective way to do your research. Be patient as you formulate your plan and make sure to take the necessary time to do the research.

Winning Point #3: Write Out Your Plan

Begin to carefully plan out each step. Write out the order of the steps. This will help you to know who to bring in if others are needed. Utilize all relevant information gathered from your research. The vision will seem more and more real as you move into the planning stages of each step. Case in point, I accomplished my vision for this book by using the same process.

Winning Point #4: Set Short and Long Term S-M-A-R-T Goals.

Goal setting plays a very critical and necessary role in the accomplishment of your vision. There are multiple reasons why they are important. They give you direction and get you started; they help to keep you focused and are able to detect when you are off course; they show your progress and how close you are to the finish line, etc. When developing your S-M-A-R-T goals, make them Specific, Measurable, Attainable, Realistic, and Time-bound.

Winning Point #5: Embrace Your Plan

As you go through the first four winning points, your passion and excitement will grow. You will begin to see your vision come alive step by step and phase by phase. There's a level of enjoyment and pleasure you will experience as you journey along the process. When you get small things accomplished, remember to celebrate them. It will fuel your fire and energize your efforts. I make it a point to celebrate my accomplishments and small victories with my wife and son.

Implement the Plan

"Failed plans should not be interpreted as a failed vision.
Visions don't change, they are only refined.
Plans rarely stay the same, and are scrapped
or adjusted as needed.
Be stubborn about the vision, but flexible with your plan."
— John C. Maxwell

The process above covers the necessary components in developing a winning vision. Once that is done, it's time to implement the winning plan. That is the fun and hard work part. My mind-set is to enjoy everything about working the plan. The ups and downs can always teach us something as we move step by step through the plan. However, we do need to be willing to make adjustments along the way. For example, we may need to change our major in college or close down a business that continues to not produce a profit or bring us passion anymore.

Winning takes a few key ingredients:

1. Passion
2. Love
3. Discipline
4. Focus
5. Patience
6. Humility

I found humility to be a strong and vital ingredient that is very critical to maintain throughout the winning journey. Being humble definitely keeps us grounded. One thing I continue to do after over twenty years in the Healthcare industry is to remember that my work helps people recover from medical issues. This work I do fits my personality. I care about more than just myself. I also love to see people doing well and winning in all aspects of their life. I rejoice and champion them on as they begin to experience success.

I said within myself, "If they can win at what they are doing, then so can I." I have downloaded winning into my subconscious mind. I live and breathe to win in life in all that

I do, whether it is in my marriage, serving at church, raising my son, bowling, etc. I must win. When the people in my circle of life see me winning, they may say, "I remember when he had nothing, or when his life looked like it was going nowhere." Then when they ask me, "What caused the change?" My answer is, "The Lord changed how I saw me, and my mind changed on how I viewed what I could or could not do." The winning mind-set focus started and grew from that moment and continues to grow to this day. There is no limit on what I can accomplish when I apply the winning mind-set focus to it. This is how it happened for me. Your story may be different, but focus on that winning mind-set and you will inspire others in your circle of life, too.

> *"We live in a culture that relishes tearing others down. It's ultimately more fulfilling, though, to help people reach their goals. Instead of feeling jealous, remember: If God did it for them, He can do it for you."* **– Joel Osteen**

Winning Key Points

➤ "You were born to win, but to be a winner, you must plan to win, prepare to win, and expect to win." – Zig Ziglar

➤ "Failing to plan is planning to fail." – Alan Lakein

- ➤ "If you don't design your own life plan, chances are you'll fall into someone else's plan. And guess what they have planned for you? Not much." –Jim Rohn
- ➤ "Any idea, plan, or purpose may be placed in the mind through repetition of thought."–Napoleon Hill
- ➤ We need the right people in our inner circle to advise and help us complete the goals and attain our vision. "Every man is my superior that I may learn from him." –Thomas Carlyle
- ➤ By keeping our eyes on the goal and knowing our vision is attainable through hard work and perseverance, we will get there if we do not quit or give up.
- ➤ "Failed plans should not be interpreted as a failed vision. Visions don't change, they are only refined. Plans rarely stay the same, and are scrapped or adjusted as needed. Be stubborn about the vision, but flexible with your plan." – John C. Maxwell
- ➤ "We live in a culture that relishes tearing others down. It's ultimately more fulfilling, though, to help people reach their goals. Instead of feeling jealous, remember: If God did it for them, He can do it for you."– Joel Osteen

Chapter 6

The Winning Talent

"Many times we take our talents for granted. We think because we can do something well, anyone can. Often that's not true. How can you tell when you're overlooking a skill or talent? Listen to what others say. Your strengths will capture the attention of others and draw them to you. On the other hand, when you're working in areas of weakness, few people will show interest. If others are continually praising you in a particular area, start developing it." – John C. Maxwell

One of the most important things about us knowing what our talents and gifts are is putting in the time to develop the main gift that will take us places in life. Never stop working on developing your gifts, especially the main gift.

We are all gifted or talented at something. Some people discover this early on in life while others discover it later. Some are told by others, "Hey, you are really good at this; you should develop this talent." One thing I have learned, though, if we do not continue to develop our gifts and talents, we will get passed up or outworked even by someone less gifted or less talented. When the time comes to show up at a high level, if we underperformed, then the job will be given to the harder worker with some talent who continued to develop that gift. When we know we are gifted we have a responsibility to learn all we can, develop the skills we need to achieve, and then use those God-given talents to continually move toward success. The truth is mediocre ability that is well developed and properly planted will produce a larger chance of success than extraordinary ability uncared for and underdeveloped.

Developing Our Talents

There are certain things we must do to develop our talents. First, we must discover our talents. We should evaluate ourselves to find our strengths and abilities. Our family and friends can help us do this. Second, we must be willing to spend the time and effort to learn the skills necessary to develop that talent. We might do this by taking a class, asking someone who has already developed that talent to teach us, or reading a book. Third, we must practice using our talent. Every talent takes effort and work to develop. The mastery of a talent must be earned.

To be the best or have a very high winning percentage in that area where we are gifted takes hard work. There are no shortcuts in life. The great Michael Jordan was originally cut from his high school varsity team. However, he used that disappointment to fuel his competitive nature and took the talent he had to another level. He played for the JV team at his high school and later for the varsity team. He continued to develop his talent and earned a basketball scholarship to the University of North Carolina where he won a NCAA national college basketball title. Michael Jordan never stopped developing his talent to higher and higher levels. He went on to win six NBA titles with six MVP finals awards. He is also now in the NBA Hall of Fame. He is the first African-American NBA majority owner. What a winner we have in Michael Jordan.

"If a man has a talent and cannot use it, he has failed. If he has a talent and uses only half of it, he has partly failed. If he has a talent and learns somehow to use the whole of it, he has gloriously succeeded, and won a satisfaction and a triumph few men ever know." – Thomas Wolfe

Many years ago people said Kobe Bryant was the next Michael Jordan, but he said, "I don't want to be the next Michael Jordan, I only want to be Kobe Bryant. People just don't understand how obsessed I am about winning." This great champion was determined to make his own name great and he did just that. He won three titles with the great Shaquille O'Neal and then won two more without him, proving his greatness and will to win to be second to none. This great superstar from day one had the winning mind-set and focus. He did the work it took to stay competitive at the highest level his whole NBA career. He never cheated the game or the fans. He is destined to be in the NBA Hall of fame, too.

The world of sports is a lot like business. There's training, competition, wins and losses, passion, and hard work. Just as an aspiring baseball or basketball player can find inspiration from successful business leaders, entrepreneurs can draw motivation from the world's hardest working and most dominant athletes.

If we look at the sports world, we see that working hard and continually developing your talent is the only way winning will follow you and be a part of you. These talented world-class athletes train year round to stay at top peak condition so they can perform at elite levels and be the best.

They continually strive to develop and improve the talents they know they have been given.

> **"I'm going to use all my tools, my God-given ability, and make the best life I can with it."**
> **– LeBron James**

LeBron James is considered by many to be the number one basketball player in the world at present day. He works on his fitness so he is always in top basketball condition. He sets goals and reaches them with a laser focus and superior work ethic. Wherever he goes, winning follows. He left the Cleveland Cavaliers to go play for the Miami Heat and won the NBA championship. In fact, the Miami Heat went to the finals four years in a row, and he won two NBA titles in Miami. That is not an accident. Winning follows this man because he has taken his God-given body and gifts and maximized them to the fullest. This man then set another goal to go back to his home state of Ohio to bring the Cavaliers the NBA title.

The task was huge but so was the resolve of LeBron James, his teammates, and his coaches. They made NBA history by overcoming a three to one deficit and won the title for not just the Cavaliers, but for the state of Ohio. I hope many will read this and remember the overwhelming odds he and his team overcame to become NBA champions. Everyone on that team was focused and led by Lebron James who is a flat out superstar of the highest order. He is talented, but I know this man will be working on his jump shot to perfect it and become even more unstoppable as a basketball player. His hard work and dedication is to be admired and hopefully duplicated by many. Lebron James is an inspiration to many including myself.

Serena Williams is an extraordinary athlete. She is getting better it seems in the twilight of her outstanding tennis career. In her I see all the "grit and grind it out stuff" that makes winning possible. I love her passion in the heat of battle on the tennis court. She started playing tennis as a young girl with her older sister Venus, who helped to develop the talent in this remarkable tennis player. They also received great coaching from their father who continually encouraged both of them to develop their talents and skills.

I knew Serena would one day beat her big sister who was on top of the tennis world for a good while. I saw the winning mind-set focus in her. Serena did overcome that hurdle. The Australian Open had just finished and Serena beat her big sister Venus who is amazing in her own right for overcoming health issues to getting to the finals. Serena also just passed an all-time great in Steffi Graf who has twenty-two Grand Slam titles. Serena now has twenty-three Grand Slam titles. The top record is held by Margaret Court at twenty-four, and I suspect Serena will hit at least twenty-five major titles becoming the greatest women's tennis player of all time. She will do it with the winning mind-set focus. She is a superior tennis player and destined to be named the best of all time.

The point is, when things get hard and seem impossible at times, we all need to dig deep, take a look in the mirror, and say, "I will overcome this challenge and win one day. I will do what is needed to develop the talent I have to become the best I can possibly be." We need to be intentional in the actions that will take us to that next level.

To be intentional is to plan out what actions it will take to improve and continually develop our God-given gift and talents.

Some great athletes have had to overcome handicaps before they were able to develop their talents and reach their fullest potential. Shelly Mann is one example of many. "At the age of five she had polio. Her parents took her daily to a swimming pool where they hoped the water would help hold her arms up as she tried to use them again. When she could lift her arms out of the water with her own power, she cried for joy. Then her goal was to swim the width of the pool, then the length, then several lengths. She kept on trying, swimming, enduring, day after day after day, until she won the [Olympic] gold medal for the butterfly stroke — one of the most difficult of all swimming strokes" (Marvin J. Ashton, in Conference Report, Apr. 1975, 127; or Ensign, May 1975, 86).

Superior athletes work hard at keeping their talents sharp, and it pays off in huge ways. Those of us who are not athletes need to understand that whatever we do for a living, we should always be the best and at the top of our professional world. We need to regularly read and gain as much knowledge as possible to stay sharp and ahead of the game.

"We cannot become what we need by remaining what we are." – John C. Maxwell

I have been overseas and have seen poverty where people would dig in the garbage to find things to sell so that they are able to buy food. I have seen a mother walk five miles for a bucket of water for her thirsty children. When those types of people get a chance to come to America, they take full advantage of whatever job or business opportunity comes their way. They will pile into a small house, make a plan to save money for a business, work twelve to four-teen hours, and outwork others to get promoted. At some point, they will reach their goals because they are not going to let this chance slip by. Going back to where they came from is not an option. The winning focus is in full affect in these people. We can all learn and be inspired by their determination to be a success in life in spite of where they have come from and the seemingly insurmountable obsta-cles they must overcome.

Winning will cost you, but what a legacy we can leave behind for our children and others to use as a blueprint to model for success.

Winning Key Points

"Many times we take our talents for granted. We think because we can do something well, anyone can. Often that's not true. How can you tell when you're overlooking a skill or talent? Listen to what others say. Your strengths will capture the attention of others and draw them to you. On the other hand, when you're working in areas of weakness, few people will show interest. If others are continually

praising you in a particular area, start developing it." – John C. Maxwell

> We need to discover those talents and then be willing to spend the time and effort to learn the skills necessary to develop those talents. Then we must practice using our talents.

> "If a man has a talent and cannot use it, he has failed. If he has a talent and uses only half of it, he has partly failed. If he has a talent and learns somehow to use the whole of it, he has gloriously succeeded, and won a satisfaction and a triumph few men ever know." – Thomas Wolfe

> "I'm going to use all my tools, my God-given ability, and make the best life I can with it." – LeBron James

> To be intentional is to plan out what actions it will take to improve and continually develop our God-given gift and talents.

> "We cannot become what we need by remaining what we are." – John C. Maxwell

> Winning will cost you, but what a legacy we can leave behind for our children and others to use as a blueprint to model for success.

Chapter 7

The Winning Mind-set

"Honestly, being a 5'11" quarterback, not too many people think that you can play in the National Football League. I knew that my height doesn't define my skill set. I believed in my talent. I believed in what God gave me. I believed in the knowledge that I have of the game." – Super Bowl Winner Russell Wilson, Seattle Seahawks Quarterback

I really want to dedicate this chapter to the eighteen to thirty-five year old age group because I see a huge difference between my era of the seventies, eighties, and nineties to this present era. I grew up understanding hard work and sacrifice would lead to success. Today, it seems like there is only a small number of this younger generation who understands the importance of hard work and sacrifice.

There seems to be a mind-set of "give me," "I deserve this," or they are just unwilling to work hard. Some don't even care to be the best at doing a particular job, if they even want to work at all. I recently read the formula below and believe it is something every generation can benefit from.

Growth + Grit + Giving = Change the World

"I don't have the research to prove it, but my gut says that the people who radically change our world for the better combine all three of these traits," says Bruce Kasanoff. "They build schools, attack poverty, and lead companies with a sense of purpose. The most exciting part of these three traits is that they all are within your grasp. You can decide to adopt them. It doesn't matter if you are rich or poor, a genius or of average intelligence. If you set your mind to embrace this formula, you will change what you are capable of accomplishing. More importantly, you will change what others are capable of accomplishing."[3]

"Mentors, by far, are the most important aspects of businesses." – Daymond John

---

[3] Bruce Kasanoff *is a ghostwriter for thought leaders.*

I work with a lot of the younger generation and encourage them to strive at becoming the best in whatever they decide to do for a living. I inspire them to find something that will give them passion and fire of which will help them to become the greatest in that field. It is the older generation's job to reach back and care enough to show the younger generation that the way to success is hard, smart work.

The technology age we live in today is something the older generation must keep in mind as well. This younger generation will have things a little easier because of it. We must show them even with all these technological advantages, the work ethic and commitment to the job will always be a top priority to their employers. This technology age can really be an added benefit as long as the drive to be the best is present and taught by parents, mentors, and leaders to this generation. Through me interacting and motivating these young people, I am starting to discover that our millennials are having the desire and drive to be winners. They are beginning to see that no matter what job or profession they get into, how important it is to find what their passion is and go after it.

As parents and leaders, we must all do a better job of teaching this upcoming generation how to win in life. Now that being said, there are a lot of great things being done by this generation, Facebook being a huge benefit for most of the world was created by a young man named Mark Zuckerberg.

Mark Zuckerberg was a computer programmer by the age of twelve. While a sophomore at Harvard, he co-founded Facebook out of his dorm room. He is now CEO of the world's largest social-networking website making Zuckerberg one of the world's youngest billionaires. "I got my first computer in the sixth grade or so," Mark says. "As soon as I got it, I was interested in finding out how it worked and how the programs worked and then figuring out how to write programs at just deeper and deeper levels within the system."

"I feel that the best companies are started not because the founder wanted a company but because the founder wanted to change the world... If you decide you want to found a company, you maybe start to develop your first idea. And hire lots of workers. Facebook was not originally created to be a company. It was built to accomplish a social mission – to make the world more open and connected."
–Mark Zuckerberg

You and I should always strive to make the place where we work much better than when we got there. We need to become super valuable to others around us. We never need to chase money; it will chase us if we become invaluable to whatever we get involved in. One of our primary goals should be to leave a positive legacy to the next generation.

"Most people believe that the best way to motivate is with rewards like money—the carrot-and-stick approach. That's a mistake," says Daniel H. Pink, author of *To Sell Is Human: The Surprising Truth About Motivating Others*. "The secret to high performance and satisfaction—at work, at school, and at home—is the deeply human need to direct our own lives, to learn and create new things, and to do better by ourselves and our world."

Focus and Self-Discipline Are Essentials for Overcoming Challenges

What this current generation seems to not understand is that no personal success, achievement, or goal can be realized without focus and self-discipline. This means being able to turn down immediate pleasure and instant gratification in favor of gaining the long-term satisfaction and fulfillment from achieving higher and more meaningful goals. The end result is we are able to make the important decisions, take the appropriate actions, and execute an effective and efficient game plan regardless of the obstacles, discomfort, or difficulties that we face along the way. Michael Jordan has always maintained that his greatness as a basketball player came from his desire to improve his talent through discipline and focus. It certainly worked for him, and it can certainly work for the rest of us. His greatness is so popular that I hear to this day other sports analysts saying, "This one is the Michael Jordan of football or baseball." You name the sport and Michael Jordan's name will surface as it pertains to his winning greatness. He is called the G-O-A-T (greatest of all time), because of his skillful basketball athleticism.

Thomas Edison tried over ten thousand times to make the florescent light bulb before he hit the winning formula to make it work. That's how winning is done. You take the failures and you learn from them. His mind-set was, "I now know that process does not work, next! That referral source did not send me any business after ten visits, next!" Name your situation and shout, "Next!"

If you look around you can see how people who come from some of the most undesirable backgrounds overcome odds of race, education, broken homes, and bad neighborhoods to make life bend to their **undeniable will to win.** They refuse to allow any excuses of why, who, and where they came from to stop them from having a winning mind-set and to overcome all the odds and become a huge success like Fubu founder Daymond John.

As a child, Daymond John lived in the Queens neighborhood of New York with his mom and seven brothers and sisters. While he was attending Bayside High School, he participated in a co-op program which made it possible for him to work a full-time job while still attending school. This was when the business spirit was conceived in him. Though he is dyslexic, he knew the importance of getting an education. "My parents always taught me that my day job would never make me rich; it'd be my homework."

"If you don't educate yourself, you'll never get out of the starting block because you'll spend all your money making foolish decisions. "
–Daymond John

"Fortunately, right now 'entrepreneurship' is one of the business world's biggest buzz words, and so many young people in our country are looking up to this new generation of CEO's as their modern-day rock stars," he says as he seeks to mentor today's young entrepreneurs. "Whenever you have that effect, it makes the job of promoting entrepreneurship much easier. Though I heard the word 'no' a lot, I kept on it, seeing each trip as a new chance to further the business. I know my drive. I will only stop when I am dead and I am not there yet."

> **"I still see people today who have the biggest opportunity in their face and they don't take advantage of it," says Daymond John. "It didn't matter how small or large the opportunity was, I looked at everything as an opportunity."**

In 2009, Daymond joined the cast of *Shark Tank*, a show in which John and four other business executives listen to business pitches from everyday people, and decide whether or not to invest money in their projects. Daymond has invested $7,667,000 in Shark Tank projects as of August 6, 2015.

Masters of Our Own Destiny

> **"If we are to be masters of our own destiny, we must develop self-discipline and self-control. By focusing on long-term benefits instead of short-term discomfort, we can encourage ourselves to develop self-discipline. Ultimately our health and happiness depend on it," says Essential Life Skills coach Z. Hereford.[4]**

---

[4] http://www.essentiallifeskills.net/self-discipline.html

My friend Roshann is a young woman who put herself through nursing school, worked hard as a nurse, and was promoted to nursing director as her career in nursing went forward. She later started her own Home Health Company where she hired nurses to visit patients in their homes to support their care. After only five years in business, she sold it for several million dollars. When I congratulated Roshann and asked her what's next, she said, "I am moving away to attend Med School to become a doctor." I know she will do it because she is a flat out winner. When she sets her mind to do something, she puts together a winning plan that will get her to her desired goals. I truly admire her zest for life and her zest to be a winner at whatever she sets her mind to do. Roshann went from college student to RN to business owner and after selling her business for several million dollars, is moving toward her ultimate goal of becoming a doctor.

My goddaughter, Crystal Miller is another person who has a winning drive as well. She bought her first home by the time she was twenty-five years old and was driving a Mercedes-Benz as well. Crystal was raised by a single mother who guided her to go to college to get a degree in marketing. While attending college, she worked as a cocktail waitress to pay for her tuition. She graduated and is now thriving in her career. Her mother encouraged her to look into the real estate market. Crystal is one who sets her focus, disciplines herself, and works hard to see it happen. She received her realtor license not long after making it her focus. She did all the research, got under a mentor in the business, and now she is moving a house per month in the Las Vegas area in less than two years in this business. We all are very proud of everything she has accomplished.

People like to say that America is the land of opportunity. Many travel from other countries to America and realize their dreams and I'm cool with that. However, I live here and also want to see those who are born here win in life too. Many people just settle for the status quo life; why not want more and do more! It's your birthright in America. I pray more people will rise up, and strive to change their mind-set to becoming a winner. You need to seek out and learn from other winners and become all you can be.

I recently read a book called *The Winning Mind Set* by Jim Brault and Kevin Seaman. It has really been a blessing to me. There are so many gems of information and motivation in this book. I strongly recommend that you read it. Brault and Seaman's pretense is simple. Seaman states, "We ask every athlete and coach this question. In competition, how much of the outcome is attributed to physical skill and how much is mental? The answer ranges from 50/50 to 80 percent mental and 20 percent physical. We then ask them, as we now ask you, "What do you do to train your psychological side?" Ninety-nine percent of the time they stare at us, searching for an answer. We have the answer! If you haven't tapped into the mental side, you are at best at 50 percent of your potential. This is just one example." Seaman continues, "In reality, it goes way beyond competition and into the improvement of performance in all areas of our lives! In business, academics, sales, personal relationships, career, and of course competition, the state of your mind-set will determine the outcome more than any other element."

Oprah Winfrey is my "she-ro" and her story is world known. What a person to look up to when it comes to overcoming and winning!

As I conclude this chapter, I pray you will consider rising up today to become the best you can be. In the words of the great Oprah Winfrey, "Your future is so bright it's blinding."

Winning Key Points

➢ Growth + Grit + Giving = Change the World

➢ "Mentors, by far, are the most important aspects of businesses." – Daymond John

➢ "The secret to high performance and satisfaction–at work, at school, and at home—is the deeply human need to direct our own lives, to learn and create new things, and to do better by ourselves and our world." – Daniel H. Pink, author of *To Sell Is Human: The Surprising Truth About Motivating Others*.

➢ "If you don't educate yourself, you'll never get out of the starting block because you'll spend all your money making foolish decisions." – Daymond John

➢ "I still see people today who have the biggest opportunity in their face and they don't take advantage of it," says Daymond. "It didn't matter how small or large the opportunity was, I looked at everything as an opportunity."

➢ "If we are to be masters of our own destiny, we must develop self-discipline and self-control. By focusing on long-term benefits instead of short-term discomfort, we can encourage ourselves to develop self-discipline. Ultimately our health and happiness depend on it," says Essential Life Skills coach Z. Hereford.[5]

---

[5] Ibid.

Conclusion

The Winning Rewards

They say a picture is worth a thousand words, so I hope these photos will help me finish this winning story of my life's work.

In 2002, I started in inside sales and two years later was promoted to Sales Associate. I started with little sales experience, but made a nice impact in the new sales area I was put in.

In 2004, I was recruited and then hired by Lifecare Solutions, and it all started to happen.

In 2006, I won Account Manager of the Year out of thirty-three sales representatives.

In 2009, I was the runner-up, but told my wife Lisa in 2010 no one would beat me.

In 2010, I was Account Manager of the Year again.

In 2011, I was in the top three.

In 2012, 2013, and 2014, I was number one Account Manager of the Year; back to back to back.

I believe we should always strive to be the best at whatever we do in life. I have heard people say, "2nd place isn't so bad." I cannot ever adopt that mind-set. I must win! When I come in second or third, I am never satisfied. It makes me work harder to be number one the next time. These years were the highlights of my sales and marketing career to date.

My total number one titles with Lifecare Solutions during 2006 to 2017 is five. Hard work and perseverance always pay off at some point if you never give up.

My greatest accomplishment now is writing this book. I am leaving a path for others to follow and am helping them to create a winning focus in their life and career.

A Fun Hobby

Bowling is one of my favorite hobbies that I do when not working on my job. I have a lot of fun doing it but I also compete, do my very best, and play to win. Here are a few of my competing highpoints:

Chris Slack Wins 1st Title in ABT Event at Cal Bowl; Lakewood, CA; August 2003.

Chris Slack Wins 2nd Title in ABT Event at Yorba Linda Bowl;Yorba Linda, CA; June 2004.

Chris Slack Wins 3rd Title in Donkee Tour Event at Cal Bowl; Lakewood, CA; June 2004.

Chris Slack Wins 4th Title in ABT Event at Regal Lanes; Tustin, CA; September 2005.

Chris Slack Wins 5th Title in ABT Event at Linbrook Bowl; Anaheim, CA in May 2006.

Chris Slack Wins 6th Title in ABT Event at Oak Tree Lanes; Diamond Bar, CA; March 2014.

Chris Slack Wins 7th Title in ABT Event at Covina Bowl; Covina, CA; October 2015.

Chris Slack Wins 8th Title in ABTA Event at Cal Bowl; Lakewood, CA; March 2016

Chris Slack Bowls a Perfect 300 game in the Big Bear Bowling League at Cal Bowl; Lakewood, CA; October 2016

It was a very sweet moment to win my first and second title but the third one was very cool. Winning never gets old.

I thank God for health and strength for without it, we are very limited in what we can accomplish.

At first, bowling was just for fun with family and friends. Then, I really started competing whereby the loser would buy pizza and pay for the bowling games. Though it was a lot of fun, my competitive juices needed something a bit more serious. So, I joined a bowling league at the church I was attending in 1995. I also started to get some coaching on how to throw the curve ball and many other things about arm swing, foot work, and so on. I really got into it.

All of these pictures and awards equal one thing to me: Winning happens by being intentional. You must plan to win, put in the work it takes to be a winner, believe in yourself and your talents, develop your gifts, and lastly never give up! You must tell yourself you can do it and you will do it. Think like a winner, talk like a winner, and study winner's behaviors in the area you aspire to win in.

I hope this book has inspired you in some way to become a winner and just go for it; time will pass either way.

God Bless!

Special thanks to my lovely wife Lisa and my son Chris Slack Jr.

Chris and Lisa Slack

Special thanks to the United States Military where I served for a total of eleven years; five years in the National Guard and six years in the Army in Field Artillery. The military life was hard at times, but I learned a lot during my time in service. I say to all military past, and present, thank you for your service; you make us safe and proud. I did see some action in Desert Storm during my six months of deployment during October 1990 through April 1991. I was proud to serve my country in that war. We were trained well, and the hard work paid off as we helped to liberate Kuwait from tyranny.

Interview Military Newspaper Article

This is another proud moment in my life. I was interviewed by *USA Today* during the Gulf War. This is an old news article and that old picture is me.

2A · FRIDAY, NOVEMBER 23, 1990 · USA TODAY

NEWSMAKERS

BEHIND THE SCENES WITH PEOPLE IN THE HEADLINES

▶ "Thanksgiving reminds us of America's most cherished values: freedom," Bush said on the USS Nassau, an 820-foot helicopter assault ship, where he was flown to attend religious services. The ship was in international waters; Saudi Arabia bans all non-Moslem religious ceremonies.

Accompanying the Bushes: House leaders Thomas Foley, D-Wash., and Robert Michel, R-Ill.; and Senate leaders George Mitchell, D-Maine, and Robert Dole, R-Kan.

At one stop, the presidential party waited in a chow line in a tent covered with camouflage netting, then joined all ranks of troops at plywood-and-sandbag tables. Soldiers leaned their M-16 rifles up against the tables as they ate.

Citing security, Gen. Norman Schwarzkopf, commander of U.S. gulf forces, withheld Bush's exact route but said he was within 65 miles of occupied Kuwait — which may have put him within miles of Iraqi President Saddam Hussein.

Not to be outdone, Saddam spent the last two days visiting his front-line troops, Iraqi state television reported. It said he told his troops: "Iraq does not want war but its sons will ferociously fight if it becomes necessary."

Spec. Christopher Slack, 28, of New Orleans, hopes such bloodshed won't be necessary but realizes it might. "We know we can do our job," he said. "We just want a chance to do it. It's time to do something with the troops he (Bush) sent here or send us home."

Bush, of course, offered no such timetable. What he did say as the sun set over the desert: "It was a very emotional day. These are the ones doing the heavy lifting. God bless them all."

Favorite Pro Bowlers

1. Walter Ray Williams Jr.
2. Pete Weber
3. Chris Barnes
4. Norm Duke
5. Liz Johnson
6. Lynda Barnes
7. Kelly Kulick
8. Kim Terrell Kearney

Bowling shirts: Relax Release Repeat were provided by Melvin Finner, CEO of R3 Sports Apparel
https://r3sportsapparel.com
Photography provided by Leinea Nabayan
http://www.leinea.com

Thanks for your time and attention to this book. If you enjoyed reading it, please share it with your family and friends.

For speaking engagements,
please e-mail Chris Slack at:
chrisslack55@gmail.com